P9-EJJ-351

Beautiful Beads

KATHY ROSS

ILLUSTRATED BY **NICOLE** in den **BOSCH**

Millbrook Press/Minneapolis

For Bader, who loves beads!
—KR

Millbrook Press
A division of Lerner Publishing Group, Inc.
241 First Avenue North
Minneapolis, MN 55401 U.S.A.

Website address: www.lernerbooks.com

Library of Congress Cataloging-in-Publication Data

Ross, Kathy (Katharine Reynolds), 1948–
     Beautiful beads / by Kathy Ross ; illustrated by Nicole in den Bosch.
        p.   cm. — (Girl crafts)
     ISBN: 978-0-8225-9214-3 (lib. bdg. : alk. paper)
     1. Beadwork—Juvenile literature. 2. Handicraft for girls—Juvenile literature. I. Bosch, Nicole in den. II. Title.
     TT860.R88 2010
     745.58'2—dc22   2008044441

Manufactured in the United States of America
1 2 3 4 5 6 – PA – 15 14 13 12 11 10

Contents

Use colorful fabric scraps to make your own beads.

Fabric Beads

Here is what you need:

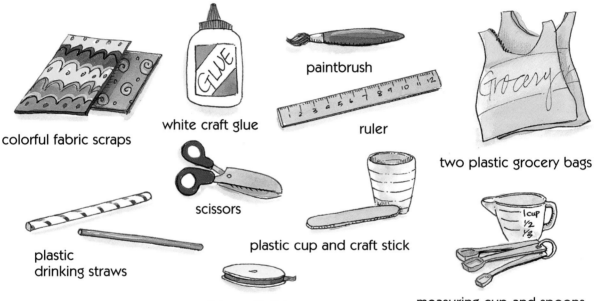

colorful fabric scraps

white craft glue

paintbrush

ruler

two plastic grocery bags

plastic drinking straws

scissors

plastic cup and craft stick

thin craft ribbon

measuring cup and spoons

Here is what you do:

1. Cut several 1- by 10-inch (2.5- by 25-cm) strips of fabric.

2. Pour ¼ cup (59 ml) of glue and 1 teaspoon (5 ml) of water into the cup. Stir the mixture with the stick.

3. Working on the plastic bag, use the paintbrush to cover a strip of fabric with glue/water mixture.

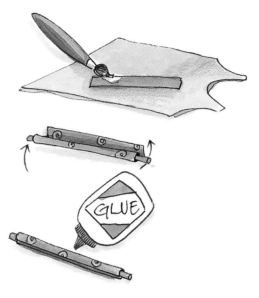

4. Roll the gluey fabric around one of the plastic straws.

5. Use more glue on the outside of the fabric to seal the edge.

6. Slip the straw out of the center of the rolled fabric. Set it on a clean plastic bag. Let dry.

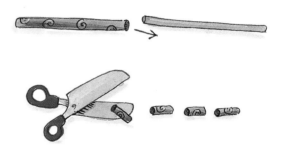

7. Make several fabric rolls. Cut the dried rolls into ¼- to ½-inch (0.6- to 1.3-cm) beads.

String your beads on thin craft ribbon, and tie the ends to make a necklace.

Give old beads a new look!

Textured Beads

Here is what you need:

white craft glue

scissors

plastic grocery bag

thin craft ribbon

ruler

wooden beads

textured yarn and trim scraps

paintbrush

Here is what you do:

1. Working on the plastic bag, cover one of the wooden beads with glue.

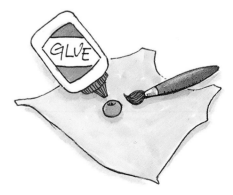

2. Wrap the bead with textured yarn or trim. Make sure you do not block the hole in the bead.

3. Secure the yarn or trim with extra dabs of glue as you wrap it around the bead.

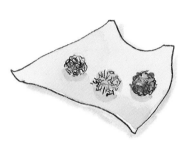

4. Cover several beads with the same or different yarns and trims.

5. Place each bead on the plastic bag. Let dry.

6. String the beads on a 2-foot (61-cm) piece of ribbon. Tie the ends to make a necklace.

You can make a textured bead necklace with just one bead or several.

Make thread beads in the colors of all your favorite outfits.

Thread Beads

Here is what you need:

plastic grocery bag

embroidery thread in a variety of colors

ruler

plastic drinking straws

scissors

white craft glue

Here is what you do:

1. Cut a 2-inch (5-cm) piece from the straw.

2. Working on the plastic bag, cover with glue ¼ to 1 inch (0.6 to 2.5 cm) of the straw.

3. Wrap thread around the gluey straw. Wrap the thread in different ways. Use different colored thread. Add more glue as needed.

4. Coat the wrapped bead with more glue to secure.

5. Place on plastic bag. Let dry.

6. Trim ends as needed so the straw does not show.

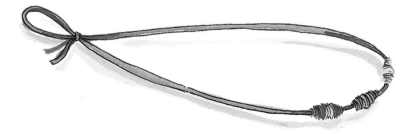

String the beads to make a pretty necklace or bracelet.

Colorful ribbons make beautiful beads.

Ribbon Beads

Here is what you need:

variety of thin ribbons

ruler

small paintbrush

scissors

plastic grocery bag

white craft glue

pony beads

plastic drinking straw

Here is what you do:

1. Paint glue onto a 1-inch (2.5-cm) section of straw.

2. Cut a 10-inch (25-cm) piece of ribbon. Wrap the ribbon around the gluey straw.

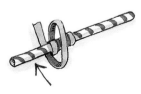

3. To wrap a second layer of ribbon over the first layer, add more glue.

4. Trim off excess ribbon. Or you can thread a pony bead on the end. Secure with glue.

5. Cover the final layer of ribbon with glue to secure.

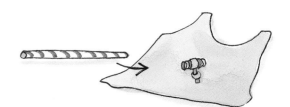

6. Slide the ribbon bead off the straw. Set it on the plastic bag. Let dry.

7. Make several more ribbon beads.

8. Cut a 2-foot (61-cm) piece of ribbon. String the beads onto the ribbon. Tie the ends around your neck.

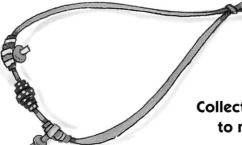

Collect ribbons of different colors and textures to make a unique and beautiful necklace.

These quick beads are bright and festive!

Sparkle Stem Beads

Here is what you need:

gold cord or ribbon

12-inch (30-cm) sparkle stems

Here is what you do:

1. Wrap a sparkle stem around your finger.

2. Slip the stem off. Shape it into a ball. Make several beads this way.

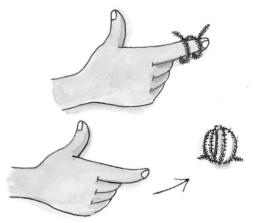

You can string the beads on a gold cord to make a necklace or on a long piece of ribbon to make a garland.

Design your own skill games.

Beads Skill Game

Here is what you need:

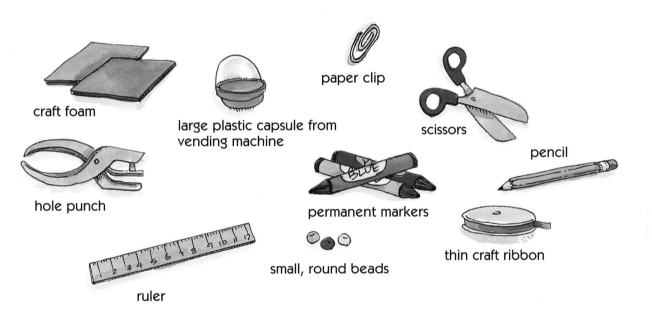

craft foam

large plastic capsule from vending machine

paper clip

scissors

hole punch

permanent markers

pencil

thin craft ribbon

ruler

small, round beads

Here is what you do:

1. Snap off the cap of the plastic capsule.

(continued on next page)

2. Trace the cap shape onto the craft foam twice.

3. Cut out the two circles.

4. Punch three or more holes in one of the craft foam circles.

5. Use the markers to draw a picture around the holes.

6. Cut a 12-inch-long (30-cm) piece of thin ribbon.

7. Fold the ribbon in half. Set it on the lid so the loop sticks out 1 inch (2.5 cm) beyond the rim.

8. Press the plain foam circle into the lid over the ribbon.

9. Press the decorated foam circle in the lid over the plain foam.

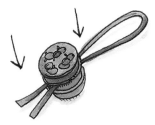

10. Drop one bead in the plastic container for each hole that is punched in the foam circle.

11. Snap the lid on the capsule.

12. Slip a paper clip on the end of the loop so you can attach the game to your coat or backpack zipper.

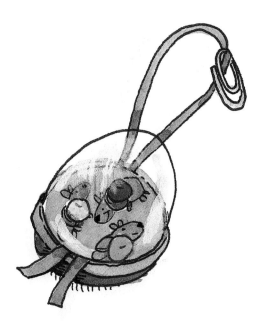

To play, shake the capsule gently to try to get the beads in the holes. For a more challenging game, hold the capsule by the ribbons and try to get the beads in the holes.

Use beads to make words, numbers, and designs with this project!

Beads Design Game

Here is what you need:

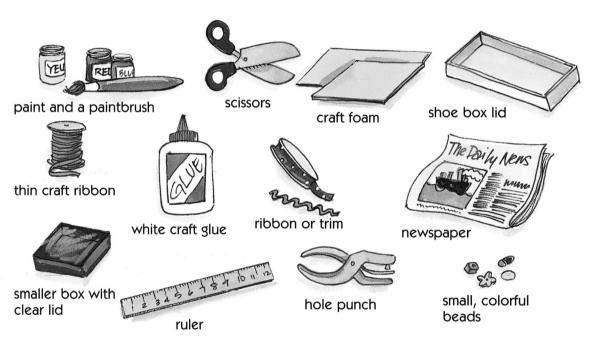

paint and a paintbrush

scissors

craft foam

shoe box lid

thin craft ribbon

white craft glue

ribbon or trim

newspaper

smaller box with clear lid

ruler

hole punch

small, colorful beads

Here is what you do:

1. Working on the newspaper, paint the inside and outer rim of the shoe box lid.

2. Glue trim or ribbon around the outer rim of the lid.

3. Cut a piece of thin craft ribbon long enough to tie around the smaller box in a bow. Tie the ribbon around the box and lid with the bow on top.

4. Glue the bottom of the box to the inside of one end of the lid.

5. Cut seven ¾-inch-wide (2-cm) strips of craft foam to fit in the other end.

6. Punch holes along both sides of the strips, as evenly spaced and close together as possible.

7. Glue the strips, side by side, in the lid.

8. Place beads in the holes to make a word, number, or design.

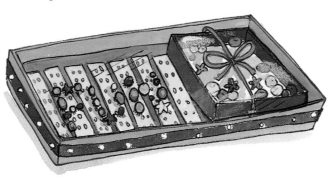

Collect a variety of small beads that rest well in the punched holes. Many of the beads from old necklaces will work well for this project. Store extra beads in the small box.

These beads make a unique and fun bracelet.

Felt Bead Bracelet

Here is what you need:

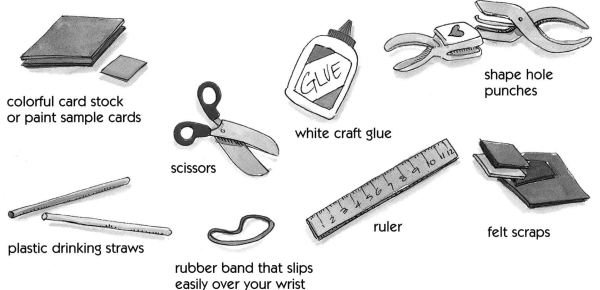

colorful card stock
or paint sample cards

scissors

white craft glue

shape hole
punches

plastic drinking straws

rubber band that slips
easily over your wrist

ruler

felt scraps

Here is what you do:

1. Cut two 1-inch (2.5-cm) felt shapes that are identical. Choose simple shapes.

2. Cut a piece of straw for each shape that is slightly shorter than the shape.

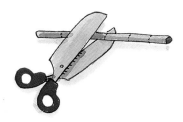

3. With the straw in between, glue the two shapes together. Leave the ends of the straw open. Let dry.

4. Use the shape punches to punch shapes from the card stock.

5. Glue the shapes onto the felt beads.

6. Cut the rubber band open.

7. String the beads onto the rubber band.

8. Tie the two ends of the rubber band together to make a bracelet.

Felt beads make great holiday bracelets. Try making a bracelet of orange pumpkins for Halloween or pink or red hearts for Valentine's Day.

This pin looks wonderful on a coat collar or pinned to a purse or backpack.

Cluster Pin

Here is what you need:

pony beads

white craft glue

scissors

four 12-inch sparkle stems

ruler

safety pin

Here is what you do:

1. Cut four 12-inch (30-cm) sparkle stems into twelve 4-inch (10-cm) pieces.

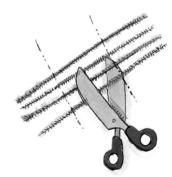

2. Gather eleven of the pieces into a bundle. Twist the last piece around the center of the bundle.

3. Wrap the two ends together to form a ring.

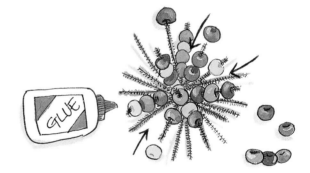

4. Flatten the ring. Slip a safety pin through the ring to use to fasten the cluster pin to clothing.

5. Spread out the stem ends to form a cluster.

6. Slip pony beads over each stem. Fold over the stem ends. Secure with glue. Let dry.

Try making a cluster pin using the fabric beads project found on page 4.

This magnet idea is "bead"iful!

Seed Bead Flower Magnet

Here is what you need:

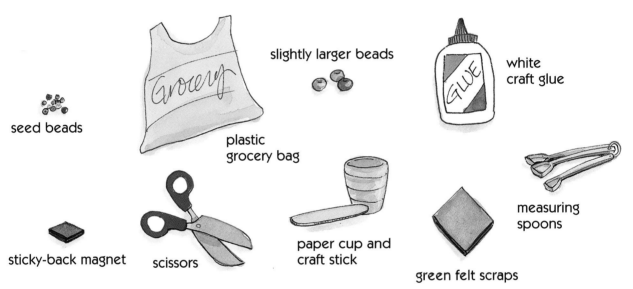

seed beads

plastic grocery bag

slightly larger beads

white craft glue

sticky-back magnet

scissors

paper cup and craft stick

green felt scraps

measuring spoons

Here is what you do:

1. Put about 1 teaspoon (5 ml) of seed beads into the cup.

2. Using the craft stick, mix in just enough glue to hold the beads together in a ball.

$3.$ Dump the bead ball onto the plastic bag.

$4.$ Press a larger bead into the center to make a flower. Let dry. Then peel the flower off the plastic.

$5.$ Cut one or two leaves from the felt.

$6.$ Glue the leaves behind the flower.

$7.$ Press a piece of sticky-back magnet to the back of the flower.

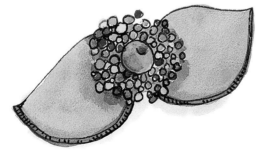

You can make bead flowers in a variety of different colors and sizes.

Beaded animals are so much fun to make that I bet you can't stop at one!

Beaded Dog

Here is what you need:

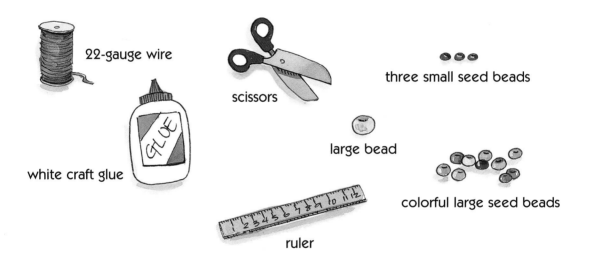

22-gauge wire

scissors

three small seed beads

large bead

white craft glue

colorful large seed beads

ruler

Here is what you do:

1. Cut a 12-inch-long (30-cm) piece of wire.

2. Thread the large bead on the end of the wire. Fold over the wire end to secure the bead head.

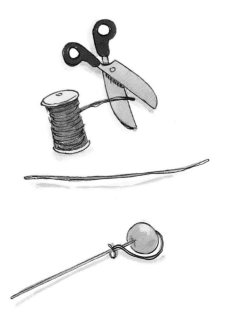

3. String some of the large seed beads onto half of the wire.

4. Wrap the seed-covered wire around itself into a ball.

5. Bring the bare wire end up over the wrapped wire to one side of the bead head.

6. Thread the wire through the bead head.

7. Thread the wire back through the body to form a tail. Trim the wire.

8. Cut two 5-inch (13-cm) pieces of wire.

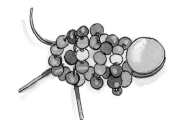

9. Thread one wire through the bottom of the body at the front, near the head. Thread the other at the back, near the tail. These are the legs.

(continued on next page)

10. Twist the wire to secure the legs. Spread the legs out so the pet will stand. Trim the ends to get the legs even.

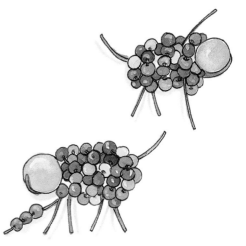

11. Cut a 10-inch piece of wire. Wrap it around the body. Add more large beads as you wrap.

12. Trim the wire. Secure the wire end by wrapping it around a part of the body wire.

13. Glue beads to the end of the legs and tail.

14. Glue the small seed beads to the head to make a face. Glue on two large seed beads to make ears for the pet.

Try making a bead turtle or a giraffe!

A spaghetti doll is a fun way to store extra beads.

Spaghetti Doll

Here is what you need:

two 30-inch (76-cm) lacing strings

two wiggle eyes

three 1½-inch (3.8-cm) beads

two 12-inch (30-cm) yellow pipe cleaners

small bead or pom-pom

ruler

extra beads

scissors

white craft glue

Here is what you do:

1. Fold one lacing string in half.

2. Thread the fold up through the hole of one large bead. Leave a 6-inch (15-cm) loop coming out of the top of the bead.

3. Thread the loop down the side of the bead and up through the bottom again to secure the string. The loop should stick out of the top.

4. Cut the yellow pipe cleaners into 4-inch (10-cm) pieces.

5. Wrap each piece around your finger to curl it.

6. Glue one end of each piece into the top of the bead for hair.

7. Glue on the two wiggle eyes and the small bead or pom-pom on one side of the large bead for a face.

8. String two large beads onto the two ends of the string hanging down to make the doll body. Secure the beads with glue. Let dry. The ends hanging down are the legs.

9. Cut the second lacing string in half.

10. Tie the pieces onto the string below the head. Let 6 inches (15 cm) hang down on each side for the arms.

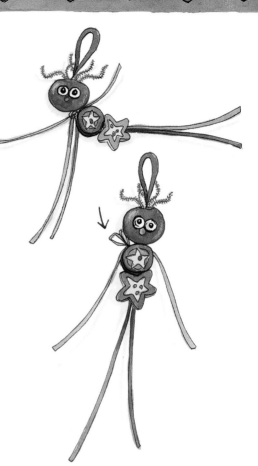

11. Tie the two extra ends in a bow at the neck of the doll.

12. Store extra beads on your doll by stringing them onto the arms and legs. Tie the end beads to secure. You can also slide extra beads onto the pipe cleaner hair.

Hang the doll by the loop at the top. The look of the doll will change whenever you change the beads.

These beaded envelopes are perfect for
storing special notes, photos, and other mementos.

Beaded Envelope

Here is what you need:

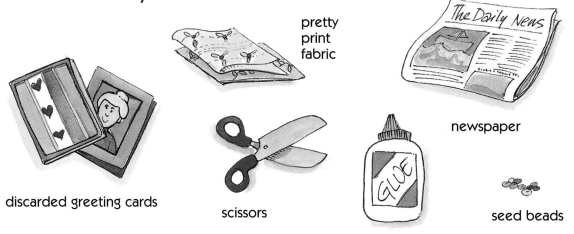

pretty
print
fabric

newspaper

discarded greeting cards

scissors

seed beads

white craft glue

Here is what you do:

1. Choose a greeting card with a
border around the picture on the front.
Cut out the picture leaving the border.
Save the picture for another project.

2. Cut a piece of fabric the size of
the greeting card.

3. Working on the newspaper, glue the fabric, print side out, to the inside edges of the front of the card, to cover the opening where the picture was cut from the card.

4. Glue together the two shorter sides of the card.

5. Decorate the fabric on the front of the envelope with tiny seed beads.

You might want to punch a small hole through the side with the opening. Thread a ribbon through the hole to tie the envelope shut.

Just shuffle the beads to give this desk friend a new look.

Changing Beads Desk Diva

Here is what you need:

discarded 6-inch (15-cm), thin paintbrush

cotton ball

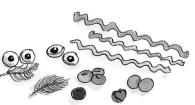

trims, pom-poms, wiggle eyes, feathers, pony beads, other collage materials

large plastic lid

scissors

white craft glue

nine or more 1½-inch (3.8-cm) beads

Here is what you do:

1. Poke the end of the paintbrush into a cotton ball.

2. Push the cotton ball end into a large bead. Make sure the cotton end stays inside the bead. Secure with glue. Let dry.

3. Glue the base of the bead to the inside of the lid.

4. Glue collage materials onto two or more beads to look like dresses.

5. Make collage faces on two or more beads.

6. Decorate two or more beads to look like fancy hats.

7. Slide two dress beads on the post, then a face bead, and finally a hat bead to build a diva.

8. Switch the beads around to give the desk diva lots of different looks.

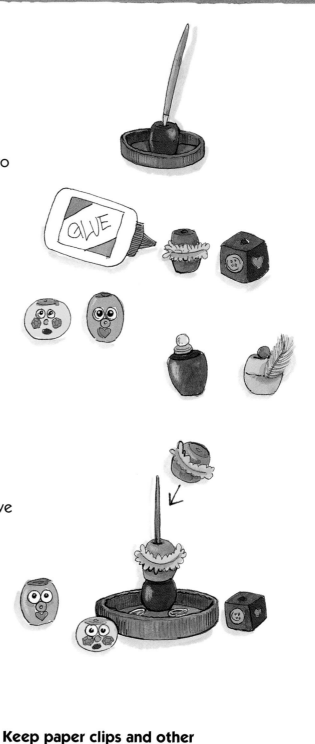

Keep paper clips and other small items in the tray of the desk diva.

Make some fancy footwear for a favorite doll.

Beaded Doll Sandals

Here is what you need:

scissors

pony beads

pencil

clamp clothespins

white craft glue

craft foam

pipe cleaner

Here is what you do:

1. Trace around each foot of your doll on the craft foam.

2. Cut out the tracings.

3. Cut a pipe cleaner long enough to wrap around the foot of your doll.

4. Poke one end of the pipe cleaner through the side of one of the tracings.

5. Thread pony beads on the pipe cleaner.

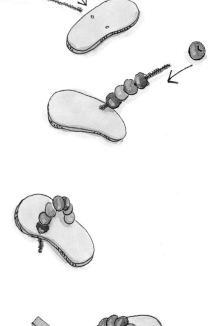

6. Poke the other pipe cleaner end through the opposite side of the sandal. Fold flat the pipe cleaner end on the bottom of the shoe.

7. Glue the identical shape over the bottom of the sandal to cover the ends of the pipe cleaner. Secure with clothespins. Let dry. Make a second sandal.

You might want to try making the top and bottom layers of the shoes in different colors.

Use this board to make bead pictures.

Beaded Picture Board

Here is what you need:

scissors

hole punch

masking tape

lots of pony beads
in different colors

ruler

white craft glue

five 12-inch (30-cm) pipe
cleaners

poster paint and a
paintbrush

corrugated cardboard

Here is what you do:

1. Cut a 5- by 6-inch (13- by 15-cm)
piece of corrugated cardboard. Paint one
side of the cardboard piece.

2. Punch nine holes along one 5-inch
(13-cm) side of the cardboard.

3. Punch nine holes on the opposite
side of the cardboard.

4. Cut the five pipe cleaners in half.

5. Stick one end of a piece of pipe cleaner through a hole. Bend back the end. Secure with glue.

6. Glue one end of each pipe cleaner in each hole.

7. Cover the glued pipe cleaner ends with a strip of masking tape. Let dry.

8. Slide rows of beads on the pipe cleaners to create a picture or design.

9. Tuck the pipe cleaner ends into the holes to secure the beads.

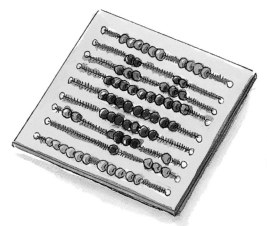

When you want to change the bead picture, unhook the ends of the pipe cleaners and slide the beads off.

Make this pretty garland for your room in the
colors of your favorite season or holiday.

Buttons & Beads Garland

Here is what you need:

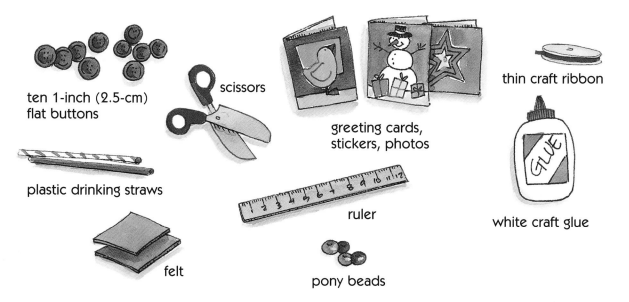

ten 1-inch (2.5-cm)
flat buttons

scissors

greeting cards,
stickers, photos

thin craft ribbon

plastic drinking straws

ruler

white craft glue

felt

pony beads

Here is what you do:

1. Cut a piece of ribbon as long as you
would like your garland to be.

2. Glue tiny pictures cut from greeting
cards, small photos, or stickers to the
front of each button.

3. Cut a circle of felt for the back of each button.

4. Cut a ¾-inch (2-cm) piece of straw.

5. Glue a piece of straw to the back of each button.

6. Glue the felt circle to the bottom of each button, over the straw piece. Leave the ends of the straw open.

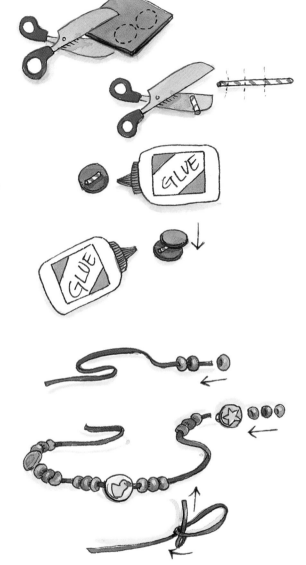

7. Thread three pony beads, a button, and three more pony beads onto the ribbon. Secure end beads with glue.

8. Leave a space between each design. Repeat until the ribbon is full.

9. Knot each ribbon end into a loop.

Each garland will be as unique as the person who makes it!

This quick craft makes a nice gift.

Beady Bookmark

Here is what you need:

thin craft ribbon

scissors

white craft glue

12-inch (30-cm) sparkle stem

ruler

pony beads

Here is what you do:

1. Fold down one end of the sparkle stem 3 inches (8 cm).

2. Cut three 10- to 14-inch (25- to 36-cm) pieces of ribbon.

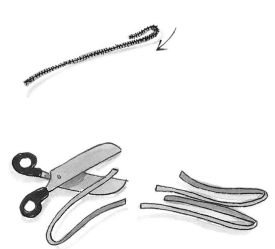

3. Bend the bottom end of the sparkle stem around the center of the ribbon pieces.

4. Fold the ribbon pieces in half. Wrap the sparkle stem around the top of the fold to force the pieces to hang down.

5. Thread some beads on the ribbon. Secure with glue.

The top of the bookmark hooks over the pages to keep it in place.

This project makes a great gift, but you will definitely want to make one for yourself too!

Beaded Tissue Box

Here is what you need:

unopened square box of tissue

newspaper

scissors

wide ribbon

pretty trim

white craft glue

seed beads

Here is what you do:

1. Remove any wrappers from the box.

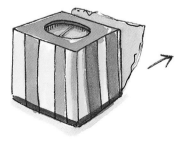

2. Working on the newspaper, glue trim around the bottom of the box to cover writing.

3. Glue seed beads to the top of the box, around the opening.

4. Tie a ribbon in a big bow around the sides of the box.

When the tissue is gone, the box can be used to store socks and other small items.

Stored beads can be prettily displayed with this idea.

Flower Jar Bead Storage

Here is what you need:

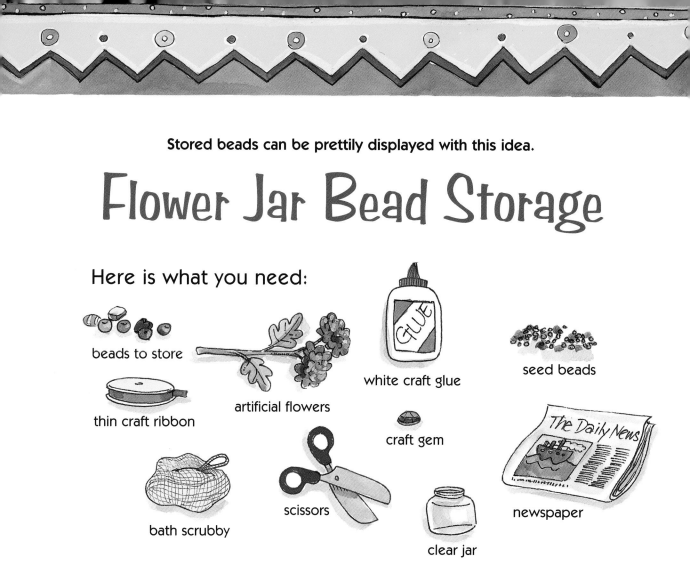

beads to store

thin craft ribbon

artificial flowers

white craft glue

seed beads

bath scrubby

scissors

craft gem

clear jar

newspaper

Here is what you do:

1. Pull the center out of one artificial flower. Separate the layers of petals.

2. Working on the newspaper, cover one petal layer with glue and seed beads.

3. Glue the craft gem in the center of the flower.

4. Glue the flower to the side of the jar.

5. Fill the jar with beads that you want to store.

6. Cut a circle of mesh from the scrubby to cover the top of the jar.

7. Hold the mesh over the top of the jar. Tie a piece of ribbon into a bow to secure mesh.

8. Poke the artificial flower stems through the mesh and into the beads in the jar.

Now you can enjoy your beautiful beads and store them at the same time!

Store your pretty beads on a stabile, and you can display them even before you use them for a project.

Bead Storage Stabile

Here is what you need:

3-inch (8-cm) Styrofoam ball

colorful beads to store

large plastic spray can cap

white craft glue

12-inch (30-cm) pipe cleaners in the colors of your beads

poster paint and a paintbrush

small stones

Here is what you do:

1. Paint the Styrofoam ball. Paint the plastic cap, if you wish.

2. Place the small stones inside the cap to help weigh it down.

3. Glue the Styrofoam ball over the opening of the cap.

4. Stick the pipe cleaner ends into the Styrofoam ball.

5. Thread various color beads on the pipe cleaner of the same color.

6. Curl the pipe cleaners around your finger.

This makes a pretty display and makes it easy for you to locate particular beads.

About the Author

With more than one million copies of her books in print, Kathy Ross has written over fifty titles and her name has become synonymous with "top quality craft books." Following twenty-five years of developing nursery school programs and guiding young children through craft projects, Ross has authored many successful series, including *Crafts for Kids Who Are Learning about . . .*, *Girl Crafts*, and *All New Holiday Crafts for Kids*.